The Little Red Wrapper

RUCHIR MEHTA

Illustrations: Bookworks.in

INDIA · SINGAPORE · MALAYSIA

ISBN 979-8-89067-653-5

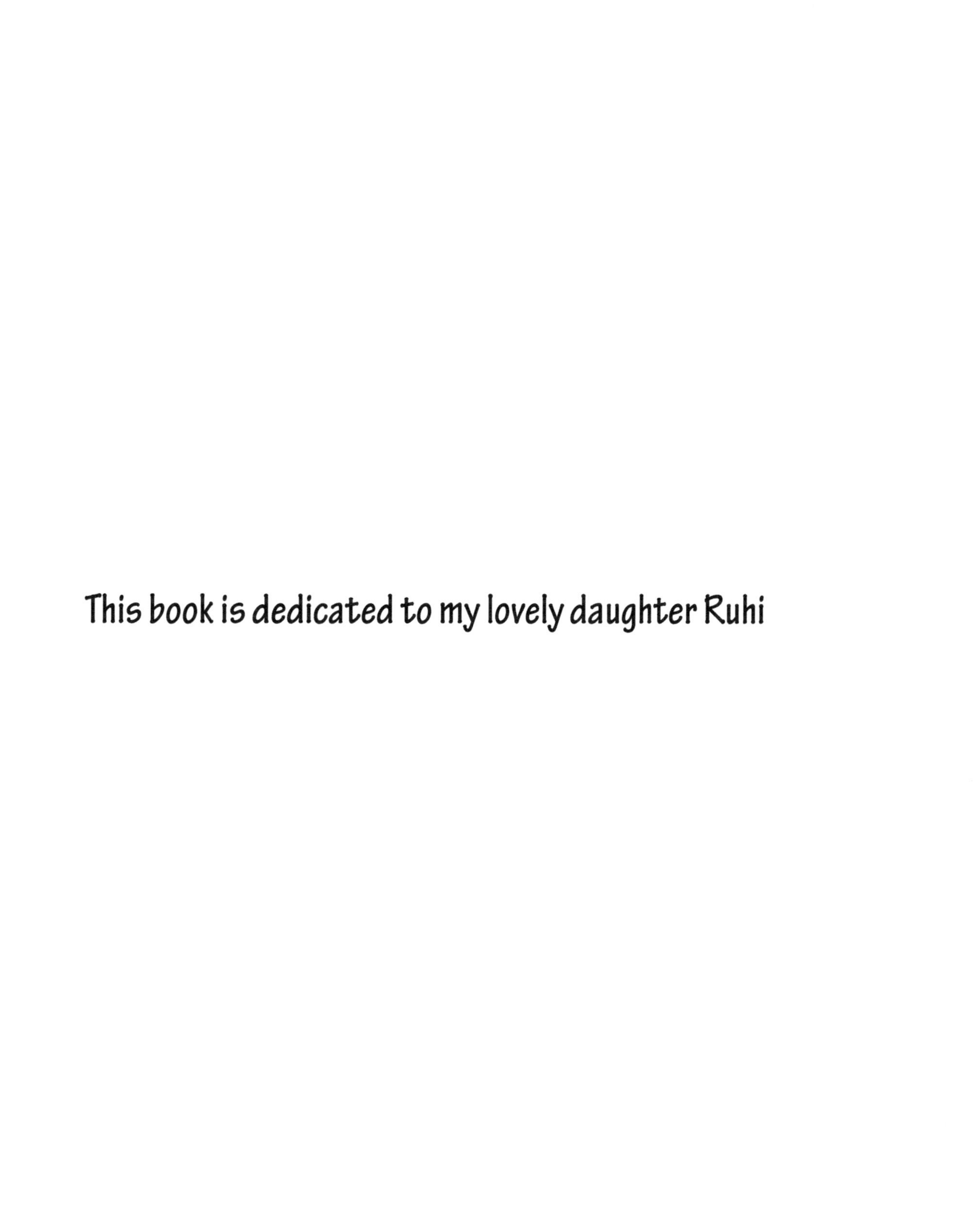

Little Selvi lived with her parents in the coastal city of Chennai. One Sunday, her parents took her to the beach. Little Selvi loved going to the beach.

She had great fun making sandcastles.

Little Selvi's mother had brought some chocolate pies for her. She loved eating chocolate pies.

Those soft scrumptious biscuits filled with marshmallows and chocolate, packed in beautiful bright red wrappers. She tore open the red plastic wrapper and ate a pie. But what was that?

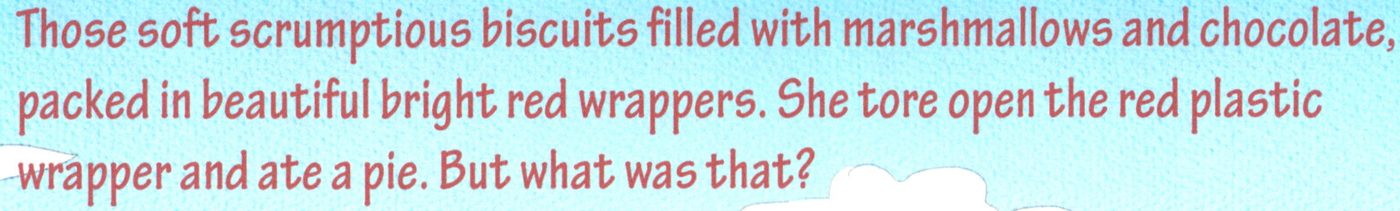

She threw the wrapper in the water. The waves carried the little red wrapper far away into the open ocean.

Kemp, a young sea turtle, was swimming in the ocean with his parents. It was time for lunch, and he was very hungry.

Kemp loved eating jellyfish. They tasted delicious. He saw something red and bright floating in the water. It was the little red plastic wrapper.

"Hey, what a beautiful red jellyfish that is," thought Kemp and took a large bite.

The piece of wrapper got lodged in his throat. He could not speak and looked terrified. "What do we do now?" cried Mommy Turtle.

"Let me think," said Daddy Turtle.

Just then they saw Mrs. Octopus swimming nearby.
"Help! Mrs. Octopus. Could you please use your many
legs to remove the wrapper from Kemp's throat?"

Mrs. Octopus tried and tried but
she could not remove the plastic.
"It is too slippery," said she.

Mr. Clownfish was passing by. "Please, help us," cried Mommy Turtle. Mr. Clownfish tried and tried but failed. "It is stuck," said he.

"Maybe we can ask Delphi, the dolphin. She is the most intelligent fish I know," said Daddy Turtle. They went to see Delphi.

"What is the matter, guys?" asked Delphi.
"Kemp has swallowed a plastic wrapper
and he cannot speak or eat. Please help us,"
said Daddy Turtle.

"Hmm, let me see. I have a couple of friends, Idea and Nelly. They
are very busy Bacteria, those two. They occasionally clean up
plastic bottles in the ocean. Maybe they can help."

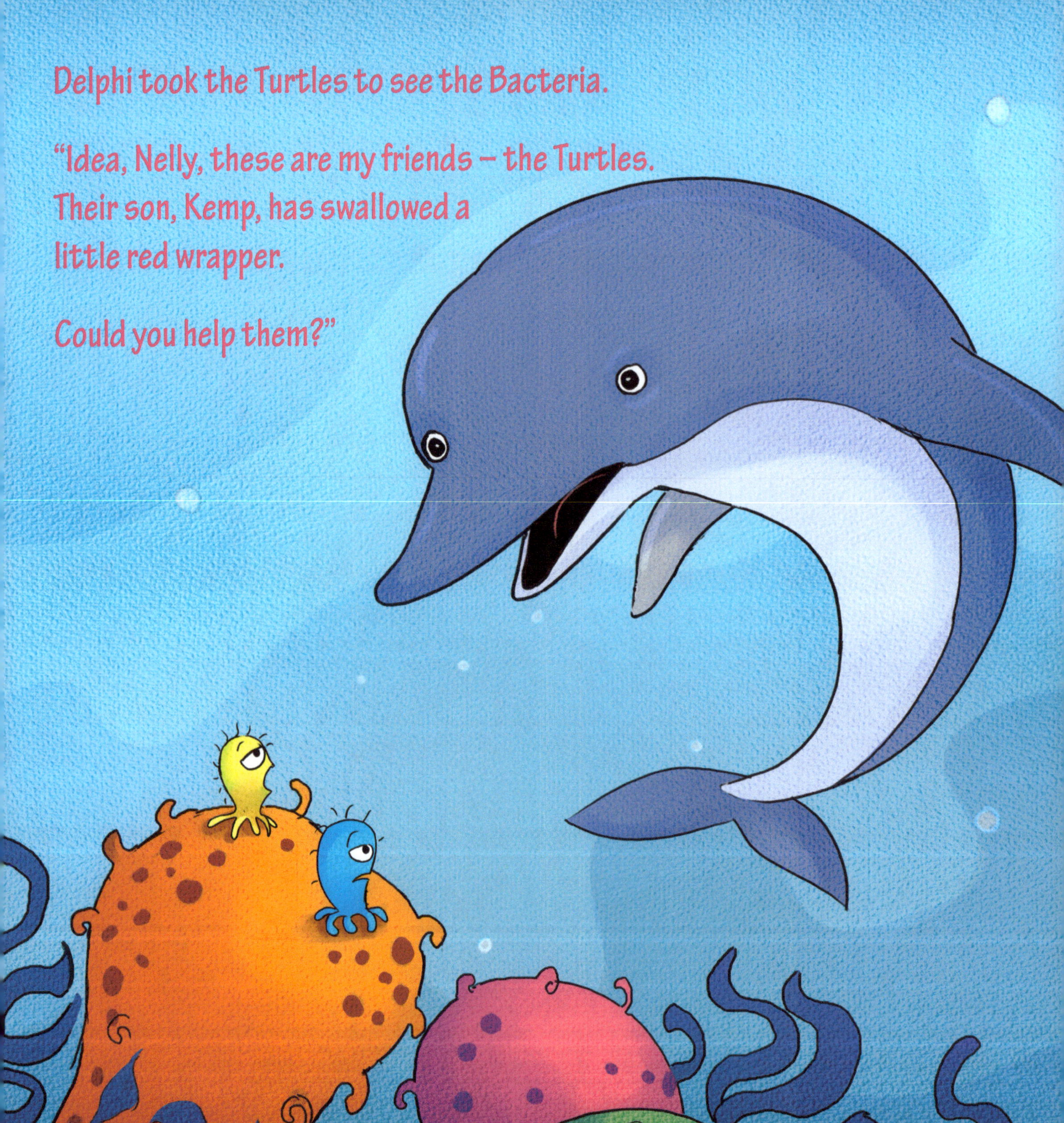

Delphi took the Turtles to see the Bacteria.

"Idea, Nelly, these are my friends — the Turtles.
Their son, Kemp, has swallowed a
little red wrapper.

Could you help them?"

"Delphi, we are old and slow. The boy will die of hunger before we clear up the plastic," said Idea.

Mommy Turtle started crying, "My baby."

"There must be another way, Idea," said Delphi.

Nelly replied, "There is my nephew, Pete."

Nelly continued, "Pete and his friends are specially trained to clear plastic from the ocean.

But his team is far away, near the coast of Japan, near that island with the spotted pumpkin."

"Let us ask Mr. Sailfish for help. He is the fastest fish I know," said Delphi.

Mr. Sailfish was so fast; he raced speedboats just
for fun.

Mr. Sailfish readily agreed to help the Turtles. After
getting directions from Nelly, he zipped away towards
Japan in search of Pete and his friends.

He had promised the Turtles
that he would try his best.

Mr. Sailfish soon reached the island with the spotted pumpkin. There, he located a group of Bacteria expertly clearing a mound of plastic waste.

"Hey, is there a Pete amongst you?"
Mr. Sailfish asked.

"I am," replied one of them.

"Your uncle Nelly has sent me to fetch you.
A young turtle's life depends on it," said
Mr. Sailfish.

"We will be glad to help, Mr. Sailfish,"
Pete replied. "You can ride on my sail,
Pete." Mr. Sailfish offered.

The sailfish carried Pete and his friends across the ocean, hoping that they could reach the young turtle in time.

"Hold on, be brave, my dear. Help is on the way," said Mommy Turtle to Kemp.

"Here they are," shouted Daddy Turtle as he saw Mr. Sailfish swimming rapidly towards them.

"Let's get to work, fellas," said Pete to his friends. They attacked the wrapper like piranhas attack their prey. They munched and chomped on the plastic. Within minutes, they cleaned up that piece of red wrapper.

"Job well done, guys," said Pete to his friends.

Kemp coughed a bit and said, "Mommy, hey, Mommy, I can speak again."

Mommy and Daddy Turtle hugged little Kemp. They thanked Delphi, Idea, Nelly, Mr. Sailfish, and Pete for saving Kemp's life.

"Can we eat now, Daddy? I am famished," said Kemp.

"Of course," he replied, and they all laughed out loud.

What a day, thought Delphi. A young Turtle nearly died, a Sailfish had to swim all the way to and from Japan, and a group of Bacteria saved the day. And all because of the little red wrapper!

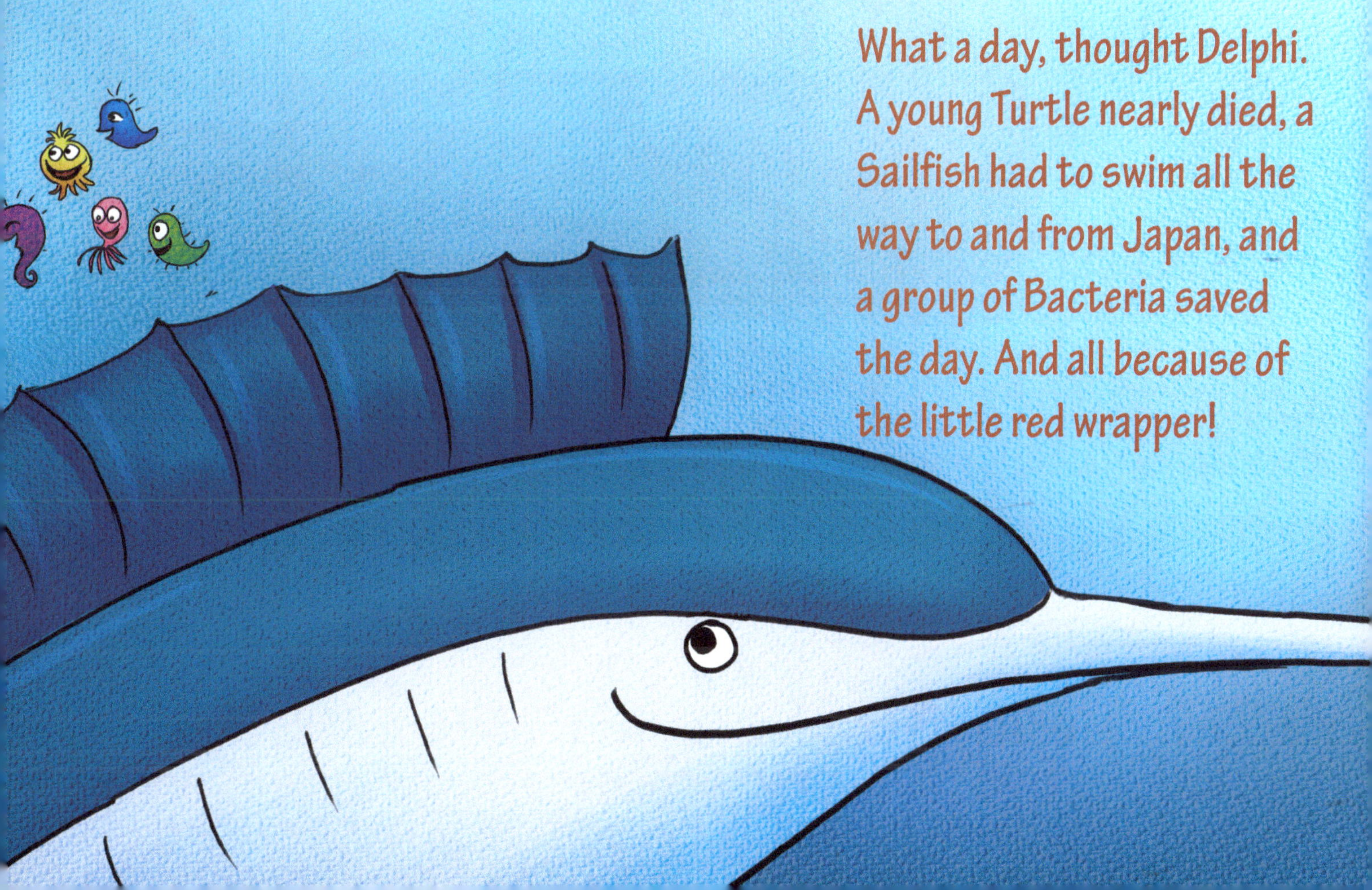